Six
SECRETS OF
A CONFIDENT
WOMAN

Six
SECRETS OF
A CONFIDENT
WOMAN

Carol Kent &
Karen Lee-Thorp

NAVPRESS

BRINGING TRUTH TO LIFE

P.O. Box 35001, Colorado Springs, Colorado 80935

The Navigators is an international Christian organization. Our mission is to reach, disciple, and equip people to know Christ and to make Him known through successive generations. We envision multitudes of diverse people in the United States and every other nation who have a passionate love for Christ, live a lifestyle of sharing Christ's love, and multiply spiritual laborers among those without Christ.

NavPress is the publishing ministry of The Navigators. NavPress publications help believers learn biblical truth and apply what they learn to their lives and ministries. Our mission is to stimulate spiritual formation among our readers.

Cover design by Jennifer Mahalik
Cover photo by Kevin Mackintosh/Tony Stone
Creative Team: Amy Spencer, Terry Behimer, Vickie Howard, Pat Miller

Some of the anecdotal illustrations in this book are true to life and are included with the permission of the persons involved. All other illustrations are composites of real situations, and any resemblance to people living or dead is coincidental.

Unless otherwise identified, all Scripture quotations in this publication are taken from the *HOLY BIBLE: NEW INTERNATIONAL VERSION*® (NIV®). Copyright © 1973, 1978, 1984 by International Bible Society. Used by permission of Zondervan Publishing House. All rights reserved. Other version used: *The Living Bible* (TLB), copyright © 1971, used by permission of Tyndale House Publishers, Inc., Wheaton, IL 60189, all rights reserved.

Printed in the United States of America

FOR A FREE CATALOG OF
NAVPRESS BOOKS & BIBLE STUDIES,
CALL 1-800-366-7788 (USA)
OR 1-416-499-4615 (CANADA)

CONTENTS

INTRODUCTION

Self-confidence or God-confidence?

"BELIEVE in yourself." That's the message of many motivational speakers and self-help books. Self-confidence.

The apostles would have laughed. Believe in ourselves? We've got no money, little education, unremarkable skills, and lots of problems. We'd be crazy to believe in ourselves. That's why we're following Jesus. We believe in Him.

Confidence means reliance, or a feeling of hope on which one relies. Confidence isn't just intellectual belief; it's belief that something is solid enough to stand on, to rely on. If we're confident in a bridge, we'll drive a car across it without fear that it will crumble and drop us into the river.

Self-confidence is the belief that we, in ourselves, have what it takes to flourish in an uncertain world. Our own abilities are the bridge we trust. Would you drive your car across that? By contrast, God-confidence reckons that we, in ourselves, have huge limitations, but that God does not. We control little, but God rules all. God is the solid Rock who can bear any weight without crumbling.

Self-confidence is the belief that we can do anything we set our minds to. God-confidence is the belief that we can do anything God gives us to do. It's not a theoretical belief, but a practical belief that gets us up out of our chairs to actually do what we feared to do before.

In this study, you'll learn how to develop and practice God-confidence. You'll learn to turn fear into faith and exchange shyness for boldness. You'll face your what-ifs and those past experiences that may have shaken your God-confidence. You'll explore the difference between true and false confidence and break free from traps like comparison, approval, and bitterness.

There's another definition of confidence: a secret told to a trusted friend, someone on whom one can rely to keep it private. Most people don't learn the secret of God-confidence because they don't turn to God as a trusted friend. Are you ready for God to entrust you with a secret like this?

How to Use This Guide

You were born to be a woman of influence. No—we don't mean a busybody or a queen bee, telling others what to do or making their lives revolve around yours. You were born to model your life on Jesus' life, and in so doing, be a model for others. Perhaps your influence will happen in a few quiet words over coffee, in a hug or a prayer. Don't say, "Not me—I'm barely treading water!" If you have the Spirit of God in your life, you have what it takes. God wants to influence people through you.

We've created these *Designed for Influence* Bible studies to draw out this loving, serving, celebrating side of you. You can use this study guide in your private time with God, but you'll gain even more from it if you meet with a small group of other women who share your desire to grow and give. The study is designed around the seven life-changing principles explored in Carol Kent's book, *Becoming a Woman of Influence*. These principles, which underlay Jesus' style of influencing others, are:

- Time alone with God
- Walking and talking
- Storytelling
- Asking questions
- Compassion
- Unconditional love
- Casting vision

Each of the six sessions in this guide contains these seven sections:

An Opening Story. When you see the word "I" in this guide, you're hearing from Carol. She begins each session with a story from her own life to let you know we're not making this stuff up in some spiritual hothouse; we care about these issues because we're living them. As you read these stories, look for a point of connection between your life and Carol's.

Connecting. Next comes your chance to tell your own story about the topic at hand. If you're studying on your own, take a few minutes to write down a piece of your life story in response to the questions in this section. If you're meeting with a group, tell your stories to each other. Nothing brings a group of women together like sharing stories. It's not necessary for each person to answer every question in the rest of the study, but each person should have a chance to respond to the "Connecting" questions. Sharing stories is great fun, but try to keep your answers brief so that you'll have time for the rest of the study!

Learning from the Master. The entire Bible is the Word of God. Yet Jesus Himself is the Word of God made flesh. The Bible studies in this series focus on Jesus' words and actions in the Gospels. You'll get to see how Jesus Himself grappled with situations much like those you face. He's the smartest guy in history, the closest to the Father, the one who understood life better than anyone else. This is your opportunity to follow Him around and watch how He did it. If you're meeting with a group, you don't need to answer the questions ahead of time, but it would be helpful to read through them and begin thinking about them. When your group gathers, ask for one or more volunteers to read the Scripture aloud. If the story is lengthy, you could take turns reading paragraphs. Or if you really want to have fun, assign the roles of Jesus and the other characters to different readers. Karen wrote the Bible study section of this guide, and if you have any questions or comments, you can e-mail her at bible.study@navpress.com.

A Reflection. This section contains some thoughts on the topic, as well as some questions that invite you to apply what you've learned to your own life. If you're meeting with a group, it is helpful, but not necessary, to read the reflection ahead of time. When your group reaches this point in the study, you can allow people a few minutes to read over the reflection to refresh their memories. Talk about the ideas in this section that seem especially helpful to you.

Talking with God. This section closes your meeting if you're studying with a group. Inviting God to enable you to live what you've discussed may be the most important thing you do together. In addition to the prayer ideas suggested in this section, feel free to include your personal concerns.

Time Alone with God. This section and the next are your "homework" if you are meeting with a group. The first part of your "homework" is to take some time during the week to be with God. In this section you'll find ideas for prayer, journaling, thinking, or just *being* with God. If you're already accustomed to taking time away from the rush of life to reflect and pray, then you know how these quiet moments energize you for the rest of your week. If you've believed yourself to be "too busy" to take this time to nourish your hungry soul, then this is your chance to taste the feast God has prepared for you.

Walking with Others. The second part of your "homework" is to pass on God's love to someone else in some way. Here you'll sample what it means to be a woman of influence simply by giving away something you've received. This is your chance to practice compassion, unconditional love, and vision-casting with the women you encounter in your daily life.

That's how the Christian life works: we draw apart to be with God, then we go back into the world to love as we have been loved.

If you're meeting with a group, one woman will need to take responsibility for facilitating the discussion at each meeting. You can rotate this responsibility or let the same person facilitate all six sessions. The facilitator's main task is to keep the discussion moving forward and to make sure everyone has a chance to speak. This will be easiest if you limit the size of your discussion group to no more than eight people. If your group is larger than eight (especially in a Sunday school class), consider dividing into subgroups of four to six people for your discussion.

Spiritual influence is not just for super-Christians. You can make a difference in someone's life by letting God work through you. Take a chance—the results may surprise you!

1

REST IN
GOD'S LOVE

*To know and feel God's love is to know the deep kind
of abiding joy that you want to splash all over others.*

—BARBARA JOHNSON [1]

MY father's first heart bypass surgery was a great success and
gave him ten more years of productive life. Then, unexpect-
edly, came the news that he needed another bypass. When he
went to the hospital, our family gathered to pray with him.

The surgeon assured us that the surgery was successful.
Our confidence soared. But then his recovery seemed slower
than anticipated. His lungs filled with fluid. For the next two
months he was in two different hospitals, seeing specialists
who now diagnosed a severe staph infection. After another
major surgery to remove the hard casement that had formed
around his lungs, he was weaker than ever. Different people
looked after him every day, with seemingly little compassion
or understanding of the work done by the previous days'
nurses and specialists. We were angry, hurt, grieving, and
helpless. Our father was dying.

Thanksgiving Day was approaching. It had always been our favorite holiday—a day when our big clan gathered for turkey, mashed potatoes, cashew salad, cheesy broccoli, Mama's carrot cake with cream cheese frosting, and Aunt Bonnie's pumpkin pie. After the meal, beginning with the youngest all the way through the grandparents, we would each share what we were thankful for during the past twelve months. But this year, Dad was in the hospital an hour away from any of our homes, and we wanted to be with him. We would definitely not be having our traditional celebration.

We gathered at the hospital and lingered next to Dad's bed, watching each labored breath. As dinnertime came, we drove down to the Holiday Inn and sat at a big table. We were in the valley of despair. My confidence in God was eroding. As we glanced at each other in this unfamiliar place, Mother reached out her precious, work-worn hands, indicating that we were all to join hands. We obliged. Then quietly, in this public place, Mother's alto voice could be heard singing softly, and we found ourselves joining in with tears streaming down our faces:

> To God be the glory, great things He has done.
> So loved He the world that He gave us His son.
> Who yielded His life an atonement for sin,
> And opened the Lifegate that all may go in.
> Praise the Lord! Praise the Lord! Let the earth hear His voice.
> Praise the Lord! Praise the Lord! Let the people rejoice!
> O come to the Father through Jesus the Son,
> And give Him the glory—great things He hath done.[2]

As I gazed into Mom's eyes, I realized she was resting in God's love—it was definitely God-confidence, not self-confidence. We couldn't fix the problem. But we could choose to confidently trust our God of love. Through that song, our Gentle Shepherd was leading us to higher ground.

Surprisingly, Dad's condition gradually improved, and he came home in time for Christmas. (That was three years ago!) In this session we'll look at a passage from John's gospel and a psalm, both of which describe God as a shepherd. We'll consider the difference it makes to our lives when we increasingly rest in God as our shepherd.

1. Take a minute on your own to read the introduction on pages 7-8. What picture, feeling, or phrase comes to your mind when you think of confidence?

2. What is one area of your life in which you would like to grow in confidence? (For example, it might be meeting new

people, speaking in front of groups, relating to men, watching your children grow up, seeking the job of your dreams, letting go of the need to control situations, or letting people know the real you.)

The key to God-confidence is knowing we are deeply loved by a God who has made the universe a completely safe place for us to live in. If you've spent much time in church, you've probably heard that God is all-powerful, all-wise, and loves you deeply. Perhaps you believe it theoretically, but how *confident* are you about it? The goal of this study is to help you become confident in your gut, where fear and embarrassment come from.

3. Read John 10:11-15. This is one of the many "I am" statements in John's gospel. What do you think Jesus is saying about Himself when He says, "I am the good shepherd"?

4. According to this passage, how is the good shepherd different from a hired hand? What will the good shepherd do if a wolf attacks His sheep?

5. What do you think the "wolf" represents in this picture? From what sort of "wolf" will Jesus protect you with His life?

6. What are some of the things in life that tempt you to question Jesus' willingness or ability to protect you from wolves?

7. Psalm 23 is one of the most familiar passages of Scripture. Its familiarity can cause us to overlook its depth. Read the psalm closely, pausing after each verse. What reasons does this verse give for *you personally* to have confidence?

Loved by the Good Shepherd

As I reflect on the Shepherd's relationship to the sheep in the first part of Psalm 23, I learn more about how much God loves me.

- "The LORD is my shepherd." That means I am the unique, personal object of His affection, attention, and care (even when I don't *feel* like He's looking out for me).
- "I shall not be in want." God loves me so much that He will meet my need—*today*—for daily care, but also to help me to experience "total contentment," not craving or desiring anything more.
- "He makes me lie down in green pastures." Philip Keller says that for sheep to lie down, they need an absence of anxiety: " . . . to be at rest there must be a definite sense of freedom from fear, tension, aggravations and hunger."[3] As my Shepherd enables me to fall asleep at night after I give my worries to Him, I experience His love and protection for me and for my family.
- "He leads me beside quiet waters." Sheep can't drink from rough, rushing streams. Each morning, I take time to drink deeply from the calm waters of God's Word and prayer, allowing God to reaffirm His love for me.
- "He restores my soul." A shepherd's term for a sheep that is turned over on its back, unable to get upright on its own, is "a cast down sheep." As women, there are many times when we feel "cast down"—worthless, unloved, and vulnerable. Keller says God's love allows us to experience the discipline of endurance and hardship—literally losing all confidence in ourselves: "If He is the Good Shepherd we can rest assured that He knows what He is doing."[4]

8. What are the things in your life that hinder you from lying down in the green pastures and drinking the still waters God provides?

9. What is one thing you can do to nurture your God-confidence?

> *It is God who loved us first. His unceasing love sends Him after us. He is the seeking Lover, the One who has made us for Himself. From the very beginning we were created to be found and loved by Him. He has woven this secret into the very fibers of our soul and when we seek Him with all the longing He has planted in our hearts . . . we simply discover Him seeking us, loving us—in all times and all places.*
>
> —SUE MONK KIDD [5]

For most of us, lack of confidence is more a matter of heart beliefs than head beliefs. Psalm 23 uses imagery to address the heart. It invites us to imagine ourselves in the scenes it describes.

Begin your group prayer time with five minutes of silent meditation on the first image of the psalm: the Lord Jesus as the good Shepherd, providing and restoring. Let the leader read aloud Psalm 23:1-3, through "he restores my soul," while the other group members close their eyes and listen. Then sit in silence and imagine yourself in this scene. Picture yourself lying down in a grassy pasture beside a lake. Repeat to yourself, "I shall not be in want." You have everything you really need to flourish. Let your breathing be slow and deep. Allow the Lord to restore your soul.

After five minutes, the leader can read the passage again and begin a time of praying aloud.

Use the remaining scenes of Psalm 23 for meditation this week. Begin with verse 3, "He guides me in paths of righteousness," through the end of verse 4. Imagine yourself being led by Jesus or the unseen Holy Spirit down a path. As the path winds into darkness, remind yourself that it is a path of righteousness and that you have nothing to fear because God is with you. Repeat the words of the psalm to yourself, and let them sink into your heart.

You can do the same thing with verses 5 and 6.

One area where many of us lack confidence is in believing we have anything to offer others from our spiritual lives. But no matter how briefly you have been walking the path of faith, you have something unique to contribute. This week, look around you for a woman in your life who is younger or newer to faith than you, or who is going through something you've been through. You don't have to "teach" that person or commit to "mentoring" her for years. Just agree with God that you're available to be present for that woman, to encourage her, to be whatever God would like you to be in her life for this season. *This season* might be a single contact with a stranger, or a friendship of a few weeks or months. It might grow into a long-term friendship. You're not on the hook forever; just agree with God to be available, and ask God what's needed.

If you're new to faith yourself, maybe you know someone else in the same boat. You may not be able to offer deep wisdom about God (yet), but you can share your thirst to know God. Make yourself available as a comrade in the enterprise of discovering God together.

> *Maybe you have a hard time believing that God likes you; maybe you don't even like yourself. But it's true. God not only loves you; he likes you. . . . Take flight and soar with Total God-Confidence.*
>
> —Donna Partow[6]

TURN FEAR INTO FAITH

*To win over fear, you must get used to living in the
"now" of faith . . . [focus] your energy on the day,
the hour, the moment in which you are living. And
as you have need, so God will supply. By faith, you
will win over fear.*

—JOHN HAGGAI[1]

I backed my car out of the garage and headed for work. As
I pulled onto a busy city street, my car seemed to be picking up speed. The traffic light ahead of me turned red, and
I put my foot on the brake. Nothing happened. In fact, my
car seemed to be going even faster. My accelerator was
stuck!

As I approached the intersection, there was a small break
in the southbound traffic. I tried to make the turn; however,
I had picked up so much speed, I hit the car that was now
waiting to make a left-hand turn, and that car hit the car
behind it. My vehicle was still picking up speed. I now had

my foot on the brake and was pulling on the emergency brake—all to no avail.

Looking to my right, I saw a telephone pole. I was fast approaching another intersection, and I realized if I could steer the car into the pole, I could avoid hitting anybody else. However, I knew that if I stayed in the vehicle, I could be killed. I carefully steered the car toward the pole and jumped out into the intersection. I saw my car swerve when it hit the curb; it missed the telephone pole, went right out into the next intersection and hit another car, and *that* car hit the car behind it. (Now it was a *five*-car collision!) My car made a circle, went up on a corner, and pulled out a fire hydrant. It climbed the curb on the next corner and hit a park bench. It did one final loop before going up on the third corner and crashing into the glass window of the IBM building on a prestigious corner in Grand Rapids.

Sirens were coming from every direction. A police officer came up to me and asked, "What happened?" I told him my accelerator had stuck and I couldn't stop my car. With amazement on his face, he queried, "Why didn't you turn the ignition off?"

I looked him in the eyes and said, "I never thought of it!"

The next day the newspaper reported, "Driverless car hits window of IBM building." Then our insurance agent called to say we had no auto insurance. Because of a mistake in our employer's office, our insurance had been transferred to another party without our knowledge. We borrowed money to pay an attorney's retainer, and the day after we sent our second large payment, he was disbarred from practicing law in our state for dishonorable reasons.

It felt like the bottom had dropped out of my life—emotionally, physically, and spiritually. I feared for our financial security and my reputation. I had no confidence in what the future held. One day when I was sunk in depression, my husband took me by the hand, and we knelt next to a kitchen chair. He prayed, "Lord, we know nothing can touch us without Your permission, and we know whatever happens to us can be for our good and for Your glory. We *choose* to have faith in You."

It was seven years before the final legal determinations were made, but in each court case it was determined that it was "a freak happening," and in spite of many legal expenses, I was declared innocent of wrongdoing or liability. I realized how often I'd started to sink in fear instead of walking in faith. In this session we'll look at what made the difference between fear and faith in the life of the apostle Peter.

1. What is one challenge you are currently facing?

Peter wasn't shy—how many people would request a chance to walk on water? But there are times when even a naturally self-confident person comes to the end of his or her resources. These are moments when the difference between self-confidence and God-confidence become clear.

2. Read Matthew 14:22-33. Describe what was going on when the disciples first caught sight of Jesus.

3. The first words out of Jesus' mouth were "Take courage!" What do you make of Peter's response in verse 28? Was this the request of faith or of folly?

4. Peter started well. He was actually walking on the water! What caused him to sink?

5. What do you think had made it possible for him to walk on water in the first place?

6. Peter's focus shifted from Jesus to the wind. Why was this a mistake?

The disciples' initial fear was perfectly normal and reasonable: they saw a figure in the dark, walking on the water; it was only natural to fear danger in the presence of the supernatural. Peter's fear, likewise, was reasonable: he was standing on open water in a windstorm!

7. Think about the challenge you mentioned in question 1. What is the "wind" in this situation—the part that would worry or concern a reasonable person? Take a moment to write it down.

8. What do you think would happen if you fixed your eyes on Jesus in this situation rather than on the "wind"?

Turning Fear into Faith

Peter was out there, walking on the water, because Jesus had called him. Jesus wanted Peter to ignore the wind and focus on Him. As I look back on the accident I had in my first year of marriage, I can see that while I was a committed Christian and knew God had called me to be confident, when the storm came, I jumped to wrong conclusions. It *felt* like God didn't care about my situation. Like Peter, I took my eyes off Him and began to sink.

Fear is a reaction to a triggering event, an event we interpret as a threat to our well-being. It can lead us to feel powerless, and that feeling often triggers rage and a frantic attempt to fix the situation. If we choose a destructive resolution for our fears, we can wind up practicing:

- *Denial.* "If I pretend I'm not afraid, my confidence will return."
- *Defeat.* "I'm a basket case! I've always been afraid and I always will be!"
- *Bitterness.* I look for a victim—an imperfect spouse, boss, or parent—anybody I can blame for my loss of confidence.
- *Escape.* My favorites are chocolate and potato chips, but drug and alcohol abuse, eating disorders, perfectionism, and workaholism are additional choices.

A constructive resolution for fear begins with *sorrow* for what has triggered the fear, which turns us to *brokenness* (where we admit we can't fix our problem ourselves). That leads to *submission* ("Lord, I can't fix my fear, but You can."). Then we are finally at a place where we can begin to make confident, faith-filled *decisions.* [2]

God doesn't want us to make foolish choices to "walk on water" without seeking His advice by reading His Word and praying for direction. But when we seek His counsel and the advice of godly people, the Holy Spirit confirms to our hearts that it's time to step out in confidence.

Faith doesn't mean bad things won't happen. The business we start in faith may fail. People we love may die. Faith isn't a guarantee against failure or suffering. Our confidence is in Jesus, not in results. Faith doesn't guarantee desirable results, although it *does* at least prevent us from sabotaging the results through our own fear. Sometimes faith feels risky, and fear feels like a "comfortable" burden—but we have a choice. The surrender that leads to faith-filled decision making is energizing and freeing.

9. In the challenging situation you're facing, which of the following responses have you observed in yourself?

- ☐ worry
- ☐ a feeling of powerlessness
- ☐ rage
- ☐ frantic attempts to control or fix things
- ☐ bargaining with God:

"If only You'd _____,

then _____."

- ☐ denial
- ☐ defeat
- ☐ bitterness
- ☐ escape
- ☐ sorrow
- ☐ brokenness
- ☐ submission
- ☐ a faith-filled decision

10. What constructive step do you think God is calling you to take regarding your response to this situation?

> *What is God calling you to do? Are you living like you believe you've been called according to His purpose? If we know who's sending us, then we know all there is to know. The rest is just details. That's the kind of faith that energizes us! Let me ask you this: Are you afraid to step out in faith to do what God is asking you to do? If so, just remember who's sending you and walk forward with Total God-Confidence.*
>
> —DONNA PARTOW[3]

Pair up with a partner. Briefly exchange information about a challenge each of you is facing. Jot a note about your partner's situation because you will be praying about it during this meeting and in the coming week.

When you're finished exchanging information, regather as a group and pray for your partner. Ask God to give her confidence in this situation. You might pray for the specific, constructive, next step she can take in her response.

Write a letter to Jesus, telling Him about something you're worried about or afraid to do. Confess your fear. Then write Jesus' words from Matthew 14:27: "Take courage! It is I. Don't be afraid." Look at those words and hear Jesus saying them to you. Write a response. Don't censor yourself; tell Jesus what you're really thinking.

Don't forget to pray for your partner.

Who in your life is facing a choice between a fearful and a faith-filled response to a challenge? How can you support this person in responding with sorrow, brokenness, submission, God-confidence, and faith-filled action?

> *Worry is a cycle of inefficient thoughts whirling around a center of fear. . . . Worry does not empty tomorrow of its sorrow, it empties today of its strength.*
>
> —CORRIE TEN BOOM[4]

OVERCOME THE WHAT- IFS

Negatively anticipating a future experience is potentially more damaging than experiencing the perceived problem. Negative anticipation is attaching meaning to circumstances or future plans on the basis of past fearful experiences.

—DR. KEN NICHOLS [1]

MY friend Amy sat in my kitchen with tears in her eyes. She was attractive, vibrant, and energetic, but I could tell something was wrong.

I poured each of us a cup of tea and then settled into a nearby chair to listen. "Amy," I said hesitantly, "I can tell something is bothering you. Is it anything I could help you pray about? I'm a good listener."

She smiled as another tear made its way down her cheek. "Well, I know I'm just being foolish," she said, "but I'm so worried about my husband and our family." Amy's tears continued as she explained that her good-looking, dynamic husband had just taken a new sales position with his company that would mean traveling to distant cities, sometimes spending two or three days away from home at a time. She said, "He's never given me one reason not to trust him, but I know there will be so many temptations when he's away. There will be other women who are longing for companionship. There's the possibility that he could watch pornographic videos in his hotel room. And he may not find me attractive anymore, and he might eventually want to leave me and our children. On top of everything, I'm afraid to be alone at night. What if someone tries to break into the house? What if they threaten me, and what if they hurt my children?"

As Amy wiped her nose, I took a sip of tea. Praying for wisdom, I slowly said, "Amy, where do you think those thoughts came from?"

A smile broke through the disturbed look on her face as she quickly responded, "Well, my mother had a great ability to worry about potential disasters. She made written lists of negative possibilities for our family. Maybe I take after her."

"Amy," I said after a pause, "that kind of thinking is *not* from the Lord. You can be sure of that! When I was a young mother, I used to have terrible fears about what might happen to my son. I was afraid to have him ride his bicycle out of the driveway; I was fearful that if he got out of my sight, something horrible would happen to him. It made me overly protective and anxious."

I continued. "My mother visited us one weekend and reminded me of a verse she had encouraged me to memorize years before. It might help you right now: *'Don't worry about anything; instead, pray about everything; tell God your needs and don't forget to thank him for his answers. If you do this you will experience God's peace, which is far more wonderful than the human mind can understand. His peace will keep your thoughts and your hearts quiet and at rest as you trust in Christ Jesus'* (Philippians 4:6-8, TLB). Why don't you try turning your worries into sentence prayers for your husband, for yourself, and for your children the next time you feel this anxiety coming on? You'll soon discover that it's much more productive to pray than to take on more worry over things that haven't even happened. Will you give it a try?"

She nodded. Before Amy left, we prayed together about our what-ifs and made a commitment to call each other the next week to pray our sentence prayers for our family members over the telephone. In this session we'll examine the what-ifs of our hearts and compare them to some I-ams, some of the things Jesus said in John's gospel about Himself.

1. Take a moment on your own to read the following list and mark any what-ifs you struggle with. Then add any other what-ifs that go through your mind regularly.

☐ What if they don't like me?
☐ What if they find out the truth about me?
☐ What if I lose my job?
☐ What if I fail?
☐ What if I'm left all alone?
☐ What if I'm not good enough?
☐ What if I lose my faith?
☐ What if I make the wrong choice?
☐ What if something bad happens to someone I love?
☐ What if they think I'm ugly?
☐ What if my kids turn out wrong?
☐ What if no one ever falls in love with me?
☐ What if I have to face that past mistake?
☐ What if I let them do it their way, and it's a disaster?
☐ What if I'm not in control?
☐ What if they laugh at me?
☐ What if my life never amounts to anything?
☐ My other what-ifs:

2. If you're meeting with a group, share one item from your list with the group.

The first thing to tell yourself about the what-ifs is a purely statistical fact: the odds of disaster are always low. If you take reasonable precautions, your children probably won't be kidnapped. Your plane probably won't crash. The pain in your stomach probably isn't cancer.

On the other hand, bad things happen to good people, bad people, all people. You *could* get cancer, and if not, sooner or later you and everybody you know will die of something. Unless Christ returns, your odds of dying within the next hundred years are 100 percent. You may try to achieve this thing you've always wanted to do, and you may fail. If not, sooner or later you'll fail at something. Everybody does. Every silver lining has a cloud, if you look hard enough.

Somewhere between paranoia and naïveté, there's a biblical way of dealing with the uncertainties of life, the what-ifs. Jesus' response is not a promise of pain-free life: they'll like you, you won't fail, you won't lose your job. His response to the what-ifs is a series of I-ams. You explored one of those in session 1: "I am the good shepherd." Here are some more.

3. For each of these I-ams, write down Jesus' literal statement of who He is and note any promise attached to the claim. Then identify what you think this I-am statement means. After that, tell how it answers the concern behind one or more of the what-ifs listed in question 1.

John 6:35; I am _____.

promise:

meaning:

what-ifs:

John 8:12; I am _____.

promise:

meaning:

what-ifs:

John 11:25-26; I am _____.

promise:

meaning:

what-ifs:

John 15:5-8; I am _____.

promise:

meaning:

what-ifs:

4. Choose your most burdensome what-if (perhaps the one
   you mentioned in question 2). What do you think Jesus
   would say, gently but firmly, in response to that what-if?

If you're meeting with a group, give each person a chance to respond to question 4. If someone has a what-if that concerns her deeply and she can't imagine what Jesus would say to it, the rest of the group can help. Be gentle! It's more important for a woman to discern what the Lord is saying to her heart than for others to come up with "right" answers.

Ultimately Jesus Himself—His identity and character, His *realness*—is the answer to all our what-ifs. No amount of reasoning can take the place of I AM.

Six Simple Truths

Sometimes we are our own worst enemy when it comes to choosing faith over fearful anxiety. There are six simple facts that will help us to face the what-ifs of each day more confidently:

- *Life is full of negative things that might happen.* Have I accepted the fact that we live in a fallen world where bad things can happen, or am I expecting life to be totally free of painful circumstances and situations?
- *As long as I choose a path of personal growth, I will face fearful situations.* Do I realize that every time I say yes to a new opportunity, a job change, a volunteer position, or a ministry assignment, I will undoubtedly face new, potentially fearful situations?
- *Acknowledging my anxieties is a positive first step.* Am I too prideful to admit to key people in my life or even to God that I'm experiencing fear? Am I trying to appear independent and totally without the need of support from other people?
- *An attitude of optimism will make today more enjoyable.* Have I found one humorous thought, anecdote,

comic, or bumper sticker today that made me laugh out loud? The Bible says, "A cheerful heart is good medicine, but a crushed spirit dries up the bones" (Proverbs 17:22). To get you started, think about this: "The people who tell you never to let little things worry you have never tried sleeping in the same room with a mosquito." [2]

- *Choosing a faith-filled decision is much less frightening than living with the underlying fear that comes from feeling helpless.* Will I face my problem (an event, situation, or person) and take progressive steps toward a daily practice of making faith-filled decisions?

- *Memorizing God's Word will help me turn my what-ifs into I-ams.* Start with Matthew 6:34: "Therefore do not worry about tomorrow, for tomorrow will worry about itself. Each day has enough trouble of its own." Write out what that verse means to you in the situation you are facing today.

Ultimately, the difference between a weak existence of living in the what-ifs and an empowered life of living in the I-ams is our personal relationship with God. Do we truly believe He is trustworthy? [3]

5. Think about the six truths stated above. Which one do you most need to take to heart today?

6. Is there anything you can do to take action on this truth? If so, what can you do?

> To me, one of the proofs that God's hand is behind and all throughout this marvelous Book we know as the Bible is the way it continually touches upon this very fear in us—the fear that we are so insignificant as to be forgotten. That we are nothing. Unconsciously, His Word meets this fear, and answers it.
>
> —AMY CARMICHAEL[4]

Begin your prayer time with praise to the Lord who *is:* the bread of life, the light of the world, resurrection and life itself, the vine from which you draw the capacity to bear fruit. Praise Him for what one of these aspects of His identity means in answer to the cry of your heart.

Lay your favorite what-if before God. Then read aloud to yourself the Scripture from this session that speaks most deeply to that what-if. Turn your what-if into a prayer.

Which of the following do you most need to do this week?

☐ Lay aside your pride, and admit to a key person in your life that you are struggling with a fear. Ask that person to pray for you—or with you.

☐ Reach out to another woman who is anxious about something. Perhaps someone comes immediately to mind. If not, be alert this week to the words and nonverbal signals of women you encounter. If you sense anxiety, ask God if it would be appropriate to have the kind of gentle conversation I had with Amy, as described in the opening story in this session. Be sure your attitude is encouraging, not scolding.

It ain't no use putting up your umbrella till it rains.

—ALICE CALDWELL RICE[5]

4

RECOVER FROM SHAKEN CONFIDENCE

When the train goes through a tunnel and the world gets dark, do you jump out? Of course not. You sit still and trust the engineer to get you through.

—CORRIE TEN BOOM [1]

IT was the middle of March and up popped a celebratory e-mail notice: "Pray. . . . Pam is in labor and we're headed for the hospital." Later in the day another announcement came through: "Pam has given birth to Emma Jean—our twelfth child! As usual, we stopped at McDonald's for breakfast en route to the hospital. . . ." The final e-mail of the day was more sobering: "Please pray. The doctor has informed us that Emmi (Emma Jean) has signs that may indicate she has Down's syndrome. We'll have the test results in a week."

Emma Jean did have Down's syndrome and Hirschsprung's disease. But the e-mail report from her parents was filled with hope, joy, gratitude to God for the birth of this remarkable child, and a supernatural peace in the middle of what appeared to me to be devastating news.

I had met Bill and Pam many years earlier while on a ministry trip to Indianapolis. At that time they had told me of the loss of their seven-month-old son, Jonathan, in a bath-tub accident. I marveled at their confidence in the God who makes no mistakes and can work everything that happens to us for our good and for His glory.

During the next few months I often prayed for my friends, but sensed a growing uneasiness in my spirit— almost an anger toward God for allowing these dear friends, who had already lost a child to death, to go through another confidence-shaking experience. I wondered what possible good could come out of allowing these precious people to deal with this ongoing challenge. At the same time, I was experiencing a family crisis of my own that caused me to question my confidence in a loving and fair God.

That day I picked up a magazine that had just arrived in the mail. As I paged through it, my finger landed on a picture of Pam and Emmi. My eyes fell on these words that Pam wrote shortly after Emmi's birth, based on what she sensed God was telling her:

You know, Pam, I only have so many Emmas to give. Some may say you were "due" because of your age, but we know better than that. Read My Book.

Every one of the children I give has "special needs."
It just depends as parents if you are insightful
enough to see what they are.

Are you available for ministry? I love you and
have not made a mistake. I'll encourage you, walk
with you, and guide your way. I have provided all
that you'll need on this journey I've given. Don't
look to others' comments, for what I am doing here
is conforming you, transforming you, as you live
out My perfect will for your lives. I'll provide for
each one in your family to share all the love they
have to give to Emma Jean. And they will learn to
love in ways they'd never have known without her.

So will you take this child I am offering to you?
She needs lots of love, hugs, kisses, and much more.
I will help you learn all the more how wholly
dependent you must be upon Me! What more could
you ask for? [2]

As I read my friend's words, I realized God was using
her unshaken confidence in a God who makes no mistakes
to restore my trust, faith, and hope in the middle of my own
family crisis. Disappointment, failure, and loss can shake our
confidence that God is looking out for our best interests. In
this session we'll look at what Jesus said to His disciples to
prepare them for a time when their confidence would be
wounded to the bone.

1. When have you experienced a setback or loss that rattled your confidence?

Jesus knew His disciples' confidence would crumble when they saw Him arrested and executed. At His last meal with them before His arrest, He tried to prepare them for what was coming.

2. Read John 16:16-33. What emotions do you think lay behind the disciples' questions in verses 17-18?

3. In verses 19-22, Jesus compared the experience they were about to go through to childbirth. How would this confidence-shaking time be like childbirth?

4. In this context, Jesus made a strong promise about prayer (verses 23-24). What did He promise?

5. Imagine yourself in a time as dark as what the disciples were about to face: their Master's death. Does the promise in verses 23-24 reassure you? Or do you find yourself feeling something like, "I asked God to keep this bad thing from happening, and He didn't. Why should I now trust Him to answer my prayer and give me joy?" Describe your response to this promise.

6. The core of Jesus' reassurance is in verse 27. When our confidence has been shaken, why is it so important to be absolutely reassured that the Father loves us?

7. In verse 33, Jesus promises that we will have *both* trouble in this life *and* access to peace from Him. If you had a friend whose confidence had been shaken by trouble, how would you help her recover her awareness of Christ's peace?

Regaining Confidence—God's Way

When our confidence is shaken, we often believe that life is unfair, God doesn't care about us, and we will never recover hope, joy, and a sense of purpose. At the deepest level, if we're honest, the focus is on us—*our* pain, *our* problem, *our* insecurity. The following truths can help us gain a new perspective:

- *Realize God has a purpose in our trials that we cannot see until we get to the other side of the pain or the challenging situation.* Christina DiStefano Davis, missionary to the Philippines, says, "God doesn't always do things the way we would do them. . . . What matters most is that our lives belong to Him, and He promises to take care of His own. . . . Stay close to Him and always follow Him, trusting He knows best. He has a special plan for . . . every one of you. Let Him shape you and mold you to be more like Him." [3]

- *Learn from your past experience.* We need to look back at what God has done in our lives during past confidence-busting experiences and learn from the way He accomplished His purpose in us and in others involved in the situation. Reflecting on the past can help us trust God in the present.

- *Take a risk.* Go out on a limb and give yourself permission to fail in order to start moving forward. Even failure is better than doing nothing. So what if you fall down? You can get up again. What's the worst thing that can happen? Momentary embarrassment? Looking inadequate? Someone laughing? Turn around and laugh at what happened, too! Then try again.

- *Internalize these truths: God is for me! He's on my side! He loves me!* You are your heavenly Daddy's little girl. If you stumble, He will pick you up and carry you. If you need encouragement, pick up His Word and hear His advice and His words of encouragement to you.

- *Tell the Enemy to get lost!* According to 2 Timothy 1:7, "God did not give us a spirit of timidity, but a spirit of power, of love and of self-discipline." That means shaken confidence (a spirit of timidity) is from the Enemy. Satan has no power over Christians, and we can—with authority—tell him to leave us alone!

The Christian life is a process of learning how to turn fear into faith, timidity into confidence, and brokenness into surrender to Him. This process of trusting God for what we cannot see leads to the daily habit of making faith-filled decisions, and it brings a peace that people without a faith-walk cannot understand.

8. Think about the five truths listed above. Which of them do you most need to take to heart today?

9. What will taking this truth to heart look like for you over the next week or so?

Thank God, the Christian life isn't about perfection. It's about process—the chronic process of God being at work in us. New lessons build on old, and that's why He tells us throughout Scripture to remember what He's already done. Our past history with Him becomes an encouragement for our present and future moments.

—RUTH E. VAN REKEN[4]

Pair up with a partner. Take a few minutes to share with her anything in your life, current or past, that has shaken your confidence in God's care for you. (If your confidence is solid these days, you can share something for which you are thanking God, but be sure you're not hiding a struggle out of embarrassment.)

Regather with the group and pray for your partner.

Jesus says many other reassuring things in John 14–16. Read John 14:18. Write this promise at the top of a sheet of paper (perhaps in your journal if you have one). Then write your response to this promise. Does it make you think, "Thank you"? "So what?" "I want to believe this, but it's really hard for me right now"?

If this verse doesn't seem to speak to your current situation, you could focus on John 14:12 instead.

Think of someone you know whose confidence has been shaken by circumstances. How can you encourage her this week? Encouragement doesn't mean lecturing her on Bible truths or giving a too-peppy hug. How can you come alongside her and feed her spirit with the peace of Christ?

> *We can live confidently because we know the end of the story—Jesus wins!*
>
> —RUTH E. VAN REKEN [5]

5

SHED FALSE CONFIDENCE

Self-Confidence looks inward: God-Confidence looks upward.

—DONNA PARTOW[1]

JOYCE was definitely having a "good hair day!" She pulled her favorite coat—knitted with large yarn loops—out of the closet and threw it on before getting into the car. Smiling confidently, she went to the grocery store and noticed that everyone in her aisle seemed to be having a good day, too. People waved and greeted her and laughed as they passed by. Even the cashier was laughing. On the way home she stopped at the cleaners and picked up her laundry. The store owner smiled at her and said, "I'll bet you are having quite a day, ma'am." She wondered what he meant, but appreciated his positive attitude. Joyce couldn't remember a day when so many people greeted her so enthusiastically.

Her next errand took her to the bank, and it seemed that

the entire waiting area was filled with people who looked her way with a smile. The teller chuckled as he handed her a receipt and said, "Hope you're having a one-of-a-kind day!"

When she stopped to fill the gas tank, once again she was amazed at the friendly people who all seemed interested in greeting her with laughter. Upon arriving home a few minutes later, Joyce walked in the back door and saw her husband in the kitchen. She said, "Honey, I've had the best day! Everywhere I've gone, people have been in such good moods, and they've been helpful, friendly, and happy. I'm really feeling good about myself!"

She paused, noticing her husband was doubled over with laughter himself. Unable to speak, he simply pointed to her back, near her left shoulder. Dangling from one of the loops on her coat was a bra. Joyce's confidence collapsed.

I've never experienced anything quite like that myself, but as a basically shy person, I have used many disguises that I thought would make me feel confident. In my twenties, my favorite disguise was *perfectionism*. I tried to please everyone—my husband, my family, my friends—by doing everything a little more perfectly than anyone else. I exhausted myself and kept others from developing their own gifts by always doing everything myself. It was my way of seeking approval and validation, even though I didn't recognize it at the time.

Then I tried being *possessive*. I tried to control my son by safeguarding him from the wrong kind of friends and from risky experiences. At times I kept him from making new friends because of my own fears of intimacy with others.

My next disguise was a *picky attitude,* which resulted in being critical of others. Then I moved on to *passionate workaholism,* thinking that my strong work ethic would hide my lack of confidence and make me look like a winner. I always flashed my plastic smile, in spite of my hidden anxieties, thinking that if I *looked* like a confident person, soon I'd *be* a confident person. But I was wrong. Much like Joyce, who believed people were friendly and open with her because she was "looking good," I, too, was basing my confidence on the wrong foundation. In this session we'll explore a variety of attitudes that can masquerade as God-confidence.

1. Do you think of yourself as having been timid or bold as a child? Give an example of a time when you displayed boldness or timidity (shyness, hesitance) when you were a child.

Some of us are naturally more timid, while others are naturally more bold. It's easy to see that a naturally timid person needs to develop confidence. It's harder to see how a naturally bold person needs to shift from self-confidence to God-confidence. As we seek to grow in confidence, it's important to recognize and avoid false confidence in all its disguises.

To those who seek God-confidence, Jesus is endlessly reassuring. However, He is not so gentle with counterfeit confidence. Our culture (both in and out of the church) rewards us for appearing confident when we're not, so it's not surprising how many of us do so. But Jesus places little value in appearances.

2. Read Luke 6:20-26. Jesus is not saying here that being poor, hungry, weeping, and rejected are desirable states in themselves. These are not things we need to become in order to earn His approval. But in verses 20-23, what *reasons* does He give for saying that His poor, hungry, weeping, and rejected disciples are blessed? What is the source of their confidence?

3. How easy is it for you to allow people to see you when you are weeping or hungry? Why do you suppose that's the case?

4. "Woe" is not a mean word; it's an expression of sadness, pity, and sometimes warning. In verses 24-26, Jesus expresses pity and warning for the rich, well fed, laughing,

and esteemed among us. What reasons does He give for pitying and warning those people?

5. To what extent do you identify with the people Jesus calls blessed? To what extent do you identify with the ones He pities and warns?

The danger of being well fed and on top of the world is that this condition makes it hard for us to notice that we're confident in ourselves and our situation rather than in God. It's easy to appear to be trusting God when everything is going well. When we have everything under control, it's hard to see how compulsively we cling to control.

6. How does each of the following grow from a lack of God-confidence?

the drive to control people and situations:

the compulsion to work constantly, the inability to rest:

wearing a cheery smile, while letting no one see the sadness or anxiety inside:

Jesus' words in Matthew 7:21-23 are enough to shake anyone's self-confidence. Jesus isn't impressed when we simply call Him "Lord," prophesy, or even drive out demons and do miracles. Only "he who does the will of my Father who is in heaven" has grounds for confidence.

7. Read Matthew 7:21-23. What do you think Jesus means by doing "the will of my Father" if He doesn't mean ministry like prophesy and miracles?

Developing God-confidence

As we grow in our relationship with God, we need to *get real*—avoiding pretense and outlandish self-confidence and also getting rid of self-degradation and self-doubts, which can grow into false humility. Here are a few simple steps for developing God-confidence:

- *Risk stepping out in faith and doing something you believe God wants you to do.* It might be to start a Bible study, become a mentor, join the worship team, befriend a nonChristian, guide a discussion group, give your testimony, or administrate a women's ministries event. If you're really shy, a risk might be just joining a Bible study. Yes, you feel afraid and inadequate, but try it anyway. Let God build your confidence as you continue to act in His strength.

- *Avoid obsession with yourself.* Two things will cause you problems: (1) self-doubt — the Enemy wants you to doubt your ability to accomplish anything good for God and others, and (2) self-glory — the Enemy will be equally pleased if you believe you are as wonderful as everyone says you are and you wind up taking the praise that belongs to God.

- *Verbalize giving God the glory when something you do blesses others.* Let people know you genuinely appreciate their thanks and that it's given you great pleasure to use your gifts for God. Get on your knees at the end of a day and thank God for what He did in hearts as you had the privilege of using the gifts He gave you. Praise Him for what was accomplished.

- *Develop a proper understanding of the gifts God gives to every Christian.* Paul tells us, "There are different kinds of gifts, but the same Spirit. . . . All these are the work of one and the same Spirit, and he gives them to each one, just as he determines. . . . Now you are the body of Christ, and each one of you is a part of it" (1 Corinthians 12:4,11,27). When we understand that none of us is more or less important because of our gifts, it takes the personal ego out of serving Him. We do what we do because it blesses the greater body of Christ, and we don't have to feel belittled or inflated because of what our job is in His kingdom.

8. What signs of false confidence (perfectionism, a plastic smile, workaholism, taking glory for yourself, and so on) and/or self-doubt do you see in yourself?

9. Think about the four steps for building God-confidence listed on page 61. Which one do you think would be especially helpful for you to focus on?

> *As our confidence in God's willingness to use us grows, we need to be developing simultaneously a God-processed view of ourselves—learning it in our minds, absorbing it into our hearts, and trying it out in our behavior.*
>
> —JAN JOHNSON[2]

Begin your prayer time with a chance for group members to confess their tendencies toward false confidence. You might allow a period of silent reflection, then let the group leader go first. Tell God how it feels for you to let people see your weaknesses. No one should feel pressured to confess something she doesn't believe is true—confession is not a time for showing off one's superior humility!

Pray over the steps listed under "Developing God-confidence" (page 61) and over your answers to questions 8 and 9. What is God calling you to be and do? If you keep a journal, write your thoughts on this subject.

It may be hard for us to recognize false confidence in ourselves, but most of us have eagle eyes for it in other people—it's so annoying! If you know someone whose false confidence annoys you, begin by confessing your attitude to God. Then pray for her to build God-confidence. Ask God to show you how to encourage her God-confidence—*without* scoring points at her expense.

Because I am loved by God, I can confess my flaws—laziness, grouchiness, self-doubt—and trust God to keep on transforming me. I no longer need to appear perfect to friends, family, and anyone who attends my high-school reunion.

—JAN JOHNSON [3]

6

Exchange Shyness for Boldness

We can be confident in our uniqueness. . . . To become the one I am created to be, isn't that my great work in life?

—Ingrid Trobisch[1]

I met Kathy soon after we moved back to Michigan. She lived next door, and our young sons, J. P. and Chris, were only a year apart. It didn't take long for them to become best friends. As our sons built forts in the woods and waded in the muddy creek, Kathy and I formed a close friendship. I admired her confidence. She had started a business that required international travel to exotic places, and as I sat at her table having tea, she would often receive phone calls from unique people all over the world. I secretly envied her bold demeanor and her assertive way of dealing with the people she did business with.

By comparison, I viewed myself as shy, reluctant to "dig in with both feet" and confidently approach some situations. I always had to know all the angles, be thoroughly up on my topic, and understand who I would be dealing with before I would ever come across as confidently as Kathy did.

Kathy seemed to have everything—good looks, a happy marriage, energetic children, and a stimulating career. However, she didn't have the Lord in her life. I started praying for her, asking God to reveal an appropriate time when I could bring up spiritual issues and talk about Christ. During the next few months we enjoyed many pots of tea together, and there were several times when I could have discussed my faith openly with her. Once or twice I tried to bring up the subject, but she'd immediately begin talking about a new age philosopher she had met and her views on reincarnation. I felt I lacked the knowledge and the confidence to defend my position when she seemed to know so much about her own positions. I rationalized that it was the wrong timing.

Several months later, Kathy told me she would be away for awhile because of a health concern. When she returned, she had lost a huge amount of weight and told me she had been fighting breast cancer. But, she said, "Everything is going to be just fine." That was it. She said nothing else about the situation. Once again, my shyness kicked in, and I decided not to ask any more questions. I thought it was something Kathy didn't want to discuss.

A month later, Chris (Kathy's son) was in our home and said his mother was in the hospital. I made plans to visit her later in the week, but the next day Kathy's husband stopped by to tell us that Kathy had passed away. I felt like my heart was beating in my throat. I couldn't catch my breath. Kathy was gone. Permanently. How could this have happened so quickly? And I had never shared Jesus with her because I was too shy to be bold in my witness to my friend and neighbor.

This was a lesson I would never forget. I made a heart commitment to become bold in my faith in spite of the shyness I had grown up with. I would never again put off sharing my faith with someone I was close to—even if it was out of my comfort zone. With God's help, I would become a bold Christian.

Research has found that babies are born with a tendency toward shyness or boldness already wired into their brains. The spiritual challenge for the naturally bold is to spend their lives overcoming pride and false confidence, while the challenge for the naturally shy is to spend their lives overcoming anxiety and low confidence. If you're shy, maybe you think pride would be an easier problem to have! Take comfort: shyness may be easier to get over than pride. In this session we'll consider what we can do to grow in a boldness based on God-confidence. We'll also look back at the whole study and think about where to go from here.

1. Over the next six months or so, what is an area of your life in which you expect to need God-confidence?

Maybe you feel nervous standing up to your boss or another powerful person. Maybe you fear being humiliated if you speak openly about your faith in Christ. Perhaps you fear being shot down if you take a stand on moral issues. Perhaps you sense God calling you to a ministry, but you're, well, chicken.

Jesus' earliest followers could be arrested and executed for serving Him openly. Thousands of Christians around the world today face similar dangers. Because He knew that death was a very real possibility for His followers, Jesus spoke about boldness and fear in the most drastic terms.

2. Read Matthew 10:24-25. Jesus says that because people call Him "Beelzebub" (the Devil), we should not be surprised if they say bad things about us. Still, many of us feel deeply hurt when someone says something ugly about us. What difference (if any) does it make to you that Jesus went through this?

3. Read Matthew 10:26-31. Here Jesus says, "Do not be afraid of those who kill the body but cannot kill the soul." Most of us are shy because we fear not physical death but soul death. What kinds of things can people do to us that *feel* like they are killing our souls? (For example: saying ugly things about us.)

4. Do you ever react in situations to protect yourself from being hurt? If so, what are some of the things you do? (For instance, in a conversation about a moral issue, you might keep quiet in order to keep people from rejecting you. Or, you might be overly pushy about your opinion in order to silence those who might want to criticize your view.)

5. Jesus tells us we should fear God (who can kill both soul and body) rather than people. How do you respond to that statement? For example, does it make you less afraid of people or more scared of being zapped by God?

6. To reassure us after that unnerving statement, Jesus talks about sparrows in verses 29-30. What do these words tell you about your Father's heart toward sparrows? Toward you?

7. Why would Jesus say fear God (because He can destroy your body and soul) but don't worry (because God values every creature, especially you)? Why does He want us to fear God and trust God at the same time?

8. What would you do differently if you knew, absolutely knew, that nothing in this life could kill your soul?

Becoming a Bold Disciple
There is a constructive resolution for dealing with a lack of confidence. The solution begins when we admit we have a problem:

- *Experience the pain.* Feeling shy isn't pleasant. It causes embarrassment, emotional trauma, guilt for not being a bold Christian, sometimes even negative physical symptoms. It's okay to feel bad about the negative effect that shyness has had on your life.

- *Turn your brokenness into surrender.* I needed to come to a place where I admitted there was nothing I could do to change what happened when my neighbor passed away before I had the courage to share my faith with her. I could wallow in my misery for a lifetime or say, "Lord, I blew it; I allowed my insecurity to keep me from being bold in my witness. Please forgive me and show me what I can do to change."

- *Look into the mirror and smile at God's creation in you.* You are a unique person, made in the image of God, "wired" with a one-of-a-kind personality, and gifted to do something significant with your life. Stop and thank Him for making you for a deliberate, important purpose.

- *Develop questions for people that don't have "yes" or "no" answers.* People love to talk about themselves, and they will think you are the most wonderful conversationalist if you ask them questions about their beliefs, occupations, passions, or interests. The exciting part for a Christian is that many of our questions can lead into an opportunity to share Jesus. A few questions that trigger interesting responses are:

  - ☐ If you had a completely free day, what would you do?
  - ☐ What would you like to accomplish in the next five years?
  - ☐ If you could meet a historical person, who would it be? Why?
  - ☐ What would you change about yourself if you had the chance?
  - ☐ Do you have any spiritual beliefs?

You'll find your shyness turning into boldness as you begin engaging in meaningful conversation that goes from the "surface" level to the "meaning" level.

- *Find a mentor or be a mentor.* If you need to be mentored in spiritual boldness, look around and find someone in your church or Bible study whom you could ask to provide a "season of encouragement" to you in learning how to be more bold in your walk with God and in your witness. If you are already bold in your faith, find someone to whom you can offer encouragement and advice.

Don't be surprised when you wake up one day and feel so excited about being a bold Christian that you can hardly wait for the next opportunity! This attitude of anticipation will produce confident words of hope for the people God puts in your path today.

9. Which of these five ideas for growing in boldness seems most helpful to you currently?

10. What is one significant thing you will take away from this study of confidence?

Confidence is not something reserved for a chosen few. Confidence comes when we risk stepping out in faith and God doesn't fail us, so we try again and wow, this great thing happens! This track record begins forming. . . .

—JAN JOHNSON[2]

In question 1, you named an area of your life in which you need God-confidence. If you'd like, bring that area to God in prayer, and invite the rest of your group to pray with you about it.

Allow each woman to thank God for one way your group inspires her to God-confidence: "Thank you that this group inspires me by . . ."

At the top of a sheet of paper, write, "Do not be afraid of those who . . . cannot kill the soul" (Matthew 10:28). Identify an area of your life in which you need boldness (perhaps the area you named in question 1). Write down any fears you have of being hurt in that situation. Write down any pain you have over your shyness. Offer your fear and pain to God, and ask for the confidence that no matter what happens, your soul's life is safe with God. Ask God to turn your brokenness into surrender.

Consider committing this statement in Matthew 10:28 to memory so you can have it available in your mind in challenging moments.

Find a mentor or *be* a mentor! To which of these tasks is God calling you at this season of your life? Step into it boldly.

> *Biographies of bold disciples begin with chapters of honest terror. . . . Fear of failure. Fear of loneliness. Fear of a wasted life. Fear of failing to know God. Faith begins when you see God on the mountain and you are in the valley and you know that you're too weak to make the climb. . . . Faith that begins with fear will end up nearer the Father.*
>
> —MAX LUCADO[3]

NOTES

Chapter 1: *Rest in God's Love*

1. Barbara Johnson, "The Greatest Joy Is His Love," quoted by Judith Couchman, *One Holy Passion* (Colorado Springs, CO: WaterBrook, 1998), p. 5.
2. Fanny J. Crosby, "To God Be the Glory" (public domain). Quoted from "PRAISE! Our Songs and Hymns" (Grand Rapids, MI: Singspiration Music of the Zondervan Corporation), 1979, p. 8.
3. Philip Keller, *A Shepherd Looks at Psalm 23* (Grand Rapids, MI: Zondervan, 1970), p. 35.
4. Keller, p. 69.
5. Sue Monk Kidd, *God's Joyful Surprise* (San Francisco, CA: Harper & Row, 1987), p. 125.
6. Donna Partow, *Walking in Total God-Confidence* (Minneapolis, MN: Bethany, 1999), p. 253.

Chapter 2: *Turn Fear into Faith*

1. John Haggai, *Winning Over Pain, Fear, and Worry* (New York: Inspirational Press, 1987), p. 305.
2. The principles in this reflection were first introduced by Carol Kent in *Tame Your Fears* (Colorado Springs, CO: NavPress, 1993), p. 31.
3. Donna Partow, *Walking in Total God-Confidence* (Minneapolis, MN: Bethany, 1999), p. 35.
4. Corrie ten Boom, *Clippings from My Notebook* (Minneapolis, MN: World Wide Publications, 1982), p. 33.

Chapter 3: *Overcome the What-ifs*

1. Dr. Ken Nichols, *Harnessing the Incredible Power of Fear* (Atlanta, GA: Walk Through the Bible Ministries, 1996), p. 30.
2. Barbara Johnson, *Splashes of Joy in the Cesspools of Life* (Dallas, TX: Word, 1992), p. 101.
3. The first five truths in this reflection were originally discussed in Carol Kent's book *Tame Your Fears* (Colorado Springs, CO: NavPress, 1993), p. 65.
4. Amy Carmichael, quoted by Judith Couchman, *Designing a Woman's Life* (Sisters, OR: Multnomah, 1995), p. 5.
5. Alice Caldwell Rice, quoted by Kent, *Tame Your Fears,* p. 53.

Chapter 4: *Recover from Shaken Confidence*

1. Corrie ten Boom, quoted by Cheri Fuller, *Quiet Whispers from God's Heart for Women* (Nashville, TN: J. Countryman), 1999, p. 70.
2. Pam Mutz, "A Gift from Heaven," *Real Family Life* (Little Rock, AR: FamilyLife, a division of Campus Crusade for Christ), December 1999, p. 12.
3. Christina DiStefano Davis, *Totally Surrounded* (self-published by Christina DiStefano Davis, Louisville, KY, 1998), p. 132.
4. Ruth E. Van Reken, "Living Confidently in a Changing World," *Virtue,* December/January 1999-2000, p. 38.
5. Van Reken, p. 39.

Chapter 5: *Shed False Confidence*
1. Donna Partow, *Walking in Total God-Confidence* (Minneapolis, MN: Bethany, 1999), p. 18.
2. Jan Johnson, *Living a Purpose-Full Life* (Colorado Springs, CO: WaterBrook, 1999), p. 108.
3. Johnson, p. 112.

Chapter 6: *Exchange Shyness for Boldness*
1. Ingrid Trobisch, quoted by Judith Couchman, *Designing a Woman's Life* (Sisters, OR: Multnomah, 1995), p. 39.
2. Jan Johnson, *Living a Purpose-Full Life* (Colorado Springs, CO: WaterBrook, 1999), p. 107.
3. Max Lucado, *In the Eye of the Storm* (Dallas, TX: Word, 1991), pp. 200-201.

For information on scheduling Carol Kent or Karen Lee-Thorp as a speaker for your group, please contact Speak Up Speaker Services. You may call us toll free at (888) 870-7719, e-mail Speakupinc@aol.com, or visit our website at www.speakupspeakerservices.com.